A SONG FOR CHRISTMAS

Ernie Richards

Dedicated to the memory of

John Hodgson

Teacher, director, writer

1927 – 1997

The best

A SONG FOR CHRISTMAS

INTRODUCTION

This is a book of songs about or for Christmas.

They cover a life-time. The first songs were written 60 years ago and the last songs just last year.

The first 4 songs in the book are completely independent.

The next 7 songs come from a nativity play I wrote called *Straw in his hair,* and the next 10 songs come from a musical version of Dickens' *A Christmas Carol.*

All are to do with aspiration, hope, love and the exhilaration that Christmas can bring.

Christmas means many things to many people.

It is first a religious event (Christ's Mass) which means it is linked to love, devotion, sacrifice and the highest ideals.It is also linked to the primitive beliefs in the need to create warmth and light in the middle of the darkness of winter. Carols help to do this.

A carol was originally a dance – a round dance, so that the group could see each other while dancing in a circle. You danced to keep yourself warm – and you could dance round a fire, for added warmth. Typical carols are: *Ding, Dong, merrily on high* and *God bless you merry gentlemen.* (As opposed to hymns which are slower and statelier, like *O come all ye faithful* or *Hark, the herald angels sing.*)

Dickens does not call his book *A Christmas Story*, which could be slow and heavy: he calls it a Carol, which is always dance-like, light and airy – and you could say, spirit-like.

Predominantly, Christmas is to do with other people: being aware of other people, whether near or far, whether family or not. Our immediate families feel the need to come together, to celebrate closeness with ourselves and with other human beings. And the need to be generous – with our families with presents and time – a scarce commodity in our busy world – and to people worse off than we are – to offer food, clothing, shelter, sanctuary, safety in a world of infinite cruelty.

Wars worldwide, diseases including Covid, starvation, floods, drought, fires, earthquakes and tsunamis: all the horrors that can be imagined.

And then the horrors that could never have been imagined: the agony of the hundreds of sub- post-masters wrongly accused of stealing money from the Post Office – over 25 years ago! The disaster of Hillsborough, the wretchedness of the Windrush generation, the unbelievable cruelty of the tainted blood scandal, the horrors of Grenfell, and all these and more taking decades to even be seriously looked at, let alone settled and justice served. And this is just our country.

Some people think that this should mean that Christmas should be cancelled – 'we can't afford Christmas this year.' But Christmas does not necessarily mean lots of expenditure. Giving time and love is far more important.

Our modern notion of Christmas is largely shaped by two periods in our history: the medieval and the Victorian.

The Medieval Mystery Play Cycles – notably from York, Chester, Wakefield and Towneley – presented a series of short plays showing world history from Adam and Eve to the Last Judgement, and highlighted the birth and the death and resurrection of Jesus – were performed in the streets of towns and became the basis of Tudor and Jacobean drama. They were written and acted by ordinary people and watched by ordinary people.

The Victorians largely created most of the things we now associate with Christmas. Prince Albert introduced the Christmas tree; Christmas crackers were invented as were Christmas cards.

And the Victorians created their equivalent to the medieval drama with their melodramas, their music halls, and their pantomimes.

Melodrama brought ordinary people the excitement of action, the playing on emotions such as fear, sympathy and compassion. Music halls and pantomimes brought comedy, sometimes very crude, dance routines, big choral numbers, exotic stories, and a lust for life. Again, audiences were predominantly 'ordinary people', which means basically poor people, who needed something out of the ordinary to give life some meaning and some real enjoyment.

The addition of songs and music takes the story to a new level.

The plots of operas and musicals are often trite and pedestrian. It is the songs which lift the words into another dimension. Think of the effect of hearing *Bring him home* from *Les Misérables* or *There's a place somewhere* from *West Side Story* or *You'll never walk alone* from *Carousel* or *Tell me it's not true* from *Blood Brothers*.

Adding songs to what is a traditional nativity play, and adding songs to the Victorian *A Christmas Carol* hopefully extends and deepens the feelings in the plays themselves.

This is what I have tried to do with these two pieces, and because not many people will ever see performances of these musicals, supplying the words of the songs at least introduces them to two Christmas celebrations that can help warm up our winters.

Ernie Richards

February 2024

JINGLE FOR JONATHAN

– who was born on Christmas Day

A birthday song
Must not be long
So here is mine
In half a line:
No gift of wine
Is so divine
As good advice
Before the ice
Of social habit
Freezes out a pink-eyed rabbit
What was before a Christian child.

So here is something to remember
More precious than any gift of gold or frankincense or
myrrh:
Something closes round you as soon as you have power
to move,
To see, to hear, to feel, something stretches tight across
That surging nerve within you, troubling to be free.
In youth, skimming the ice keel of the road,
Or biting like a whip into the open wound of a storm
You'll live, wind-sifted, on a narrow spur of joy.
But round it cranks the silver of the teaspoon and the
cane
And you are emptied of your life and left
Circling like a seagull over snow,
Helpless as knickers hanging on the line.

You'll learn too many things to make your love come true
Your hope will hang upon the twisted thread of life
A glittering ring which any sleight of hand
May softly drop, and leave the thread uncut.
And so you'll live as we all live,
Creatures of a frozen joy, who know
No passion but the heart's longing.

We give you a hope on your birthday morning,
A hope that you can avoid the crush:
The back door sticks, but it isn't bolted.

But you must know:
There is a formula for this and that,
To help you when you buy a hat,
To make you walk a certain way,
And guard against the things you say,
To keep yourself well uniformed
In what the new smart set have scorned,
To guide you when you choose a wife
And tell you how to hold a knife.
This is not only for the outside things
For even inmost thoughts are clipped of wings
And taught to march in step and two-abreast
And lulled to sleep if they should need a rest.
For ministers and bosses find they're all agreed
That people shouldn't have to think when there really is no need.
The papers and the telly do it for them just as well -

If writers started thinking, their books would never sell.
And so this little code is switched on at the mains,
And is always there for you to use – to serve instead of brains.
Yet here's the thing that is so strange
That limits your ambitious range –
It's not just for the youngest few:
It's made to last your whole life through.

We give you a hope on your birthday morning,
A hope that you can avoid the crush:
The back door sticks, but it isn't bolted.

OUR LADY OF SORROWS

Lady of all sorrows

Weep for me

Lady of all sorrows

Weep for me

Lady of all sorrows

Pray for me

Lady of all sorrows

Pray for me

Lady of all sorrows

Set me free

Lady of all sorrows

Set me free

THE LAMB-KING

The shepherds knew a lamb was born,

Weak and struggling to survive

They knew he needed food to live,

Warmth and his mother's breast

The lamb would talk to everyone

The rich and poor, the well and ill

He would talk and comfort bring

And heal the sick and blind

The wise men knew a King was born

A King born to rule the earth

Heavy with the sins of the world

Pity and love for all mankind.

The Lamb-King was born to die

To give his life so we could live

All glory to the King of life

Slain by a Roman butcher's knife

ROOM AT THE INN

More wine, look lively there
And bring us food as well,
Stop dawdling and gossiping
And do your flaming job

What's that noise? That shrieking?
What – some woman having a baby?
For God's sake, is there no decency?
Where is she in the name of God?

A stable? Are you mad?
She's who? A joiner's wife?
Close the door – keep out the noise
God preserve us from all screaming brats

SONGS FROM 'STRAW IN HIS HAIR'

WHEN WILL OUR LORD APPEAR?

*John and Rebecca live in Nazareth around the time
of Jesus's birth and, like Mary and Joseph, have to go
to Bethlehem to register for taxation. They and their
children resent the Roman occupation and long for
freedom.*

Chorus

>*When will our Lord appear?*
>*When will we lose our fear?*
>*Must be wait for ever and ever?*
>*When will our Lord appear?*

Oh, will he come with thunder and with lightning?
Will the earth quake beneath his feet?
Will the mountains tremble as he passes?
Will the rocks melt with the heat?

Or, will he come so softly in the evening?
Will he come so gently in the night?
Will he come so quietly in the morning?
Silently and out of sight.

Chorus

Oh, will his voice be powerful and compelling?
Will he strike all sinners to the ground?
Will he smite the evil and the wicked?
And make all life end in a shroud?

Or, will he smile so gently in his cradle?
Will he sing so softly to his Dad?
Will he croon so quietly to his mother?
So the world no longer is sad?

Chorus

When will our Lord appear?
When will we lose our fear?
Must we wait for ever and ever?
When, when, when, when, when will our Lord
appear?

GOD'S GOING TO BE A LITTLE BABY

The children, left behind when their parents set out for Bethlehem, suspect their parents are in danger and go after them to warn them. They are frightened by meeting thieves and are reassured by meeting shepherds. An angel sings 'God's going to be a little baby'.
(As a Calypso.)

God's going to be a little baby,
Tender and mild, a little baby.
He's going to rule the whole world,
But he's only going to be a little child.

He's going to be the King of heaven
Powerful and just, the King of heaven,
He's going to rule the universe,
But he's only going to be a little child.

He's going to take our sins away,
Forgiving and kind in every way,
He's going to turn night into day,
But he's only going to be a little child.

He's going to end our strife and fury,
Make of our lives a different story,
Bring us to live with him in glory
But he's only going to be a little child.

KINGS' SONG AND DANCE

*In Bethlehem at the stable the three kings tell of
their travels, their initial rejection of Jesus and then
their full acceptance in a triumphant song and
dance.*

As the star in the East climbed higher
And shone brighter than any star before,
We knew we must leave our wives and children
And follow it to the furthest shore.

We took food and drink on our camels
For ourselves and the King we would find
Spices, silks, rugs for him to lie on,
Rich furs, heavy cloaks, all damask-lined.

Day by day, night by night we rode on,
Moving on through the rain and the snow,
We dreamed of warm fires in our own homes
And yet we knew that we must go.

At last, here's the court of King Herod
We can rest, we can live like a King
But he says he has heard of no child
Of the star, he knows not a thing.

On again, through the freezing deserts,
On again, we must never look back
Still the star keeps on moving and moving –
Till it stops over a broken-down shack.

No King would be born in a stable
With horses and cows living there
There's only a poorly wrapped baby
No crown, but straw in his hair.

This can't be the King we are looking for
He can't lie in a stable bare.
Sadly, we turn and open the door
And step into the cold night air.

Suddenly the whole street is dancing
Whirling and swirling in a mad snow storm
Men and women, children and animals
Making the whole wide world warm.

All the stars and all the planets
Turn and spin to the new-born King
And we know that this truly is God's son
And we sing and sing and sing and sing.

And we dance with all of the people,
Men and women and the children too
And lift them to the skies in their glory
And dance and dance the whole night through.

As we go back to our own country
Through the cold and wintry snows
We can hear all the children singing
We can feel the dancing in our toes.

As we come to every tiny village
Everyone turns out to see us go
We tell them all about the baby Jesus
Tell them the only way we know.

And we dance with all of the people,
Men and women and the children too
And lift them to the skies in their glory
And dance and dance the whole night through.

COME TO JESUS

The children and the shepherds arrive at the manger.
Mary sings 'Come to Jesus'.

Come to Jesus, come my love,
He will save you all.
Come to Jesus, come my love,
He will stop your fall.

Come to Jesus, come my dove
He will raise you up.
Come to Jesus, come my dove
He will fill your cup.

Come to Jesus, come my dear
For now and ever more.
Come to Jesus, come my dear
He is, he is, the core.

Come to Jesus, come my sweet
His love will overflow.
Come to Jesus, come my sweet
And share his warmth and glow.

Come to Jesus, come my dear
And share your pain and woe.
Come to Jesus, come my dear
His love is yours to show.

SWEET LITTLE BABY

The shepherds give their gifts, followed by the children.
Mary and Joseph sing a bitter-sweet lullaby.

MARY   Sweet little baby, sleep my dear
                   Sleep in peace and have no fear
                   Sweet little baby, sleep my dear
                   Sweet little baby sleep.

JOSEPH   Blow North wind blow, my darling
                   Blow North wind, blow
                   We must learn to weep, my sweeting
                   Mother's smiles turn to death's greeting.
                   Blow North wind, blow.

MARY   Sleep little baby, sleep my dear
                   We will watch over you my dear
                   Play and laugh and cry with you
                   Sweet little baby, sleep.

JOSEPH   Blow North wind blow my darling
                   Blow North wind blow
                   You must learn to suffer and die
                   In a cold sepulchre to lie
                   Blow North wind blow.

MARY   Sleep little baby sleep my dear
                   You will wake to rule in glory
                   The whole world will sing your story
                   Sleep, little baby, sleep.

IN THE HANDS OF GOD

The children return home, followed by their parents.
They all learn of Herod's killing the babies, think that
Jesus has been killed but then learn that Mary, Joseph
and Jesus have fled the country. In relief they sing 'In the
hands of God'.

In the hands of God, we can stretch ourselves,
Feel power and strength coming through.
We can plan, can move, can empathise,
We are new made in the hands of God.

In the hands of God, we have no fear,
For his love will power us through.
We can fight for the poor and the sick
And those whose joys are few.

For the world is full of sickness and pain
And children growing up all alone.
We can give them our love and our help
Because we're safe in the hands of God.

At the end of the day when our life is run
And all our light must go,
We can come to rest, to rest
To rest, safe in the hands of God.

NOEL

As a finale, and as an expression of relief and joy,
everyone sings 'Noel'.

Noel, noel, noel
Good news we come to tell
About a baby born today
In a manger in the hay
Whatever could he come to say
Noel, noel, noel.

Noel, noel, noel
The truth we have to tell
He came to save us all from sin,
To show us heaven and take us in
All our souls he came to win.
Noel, noel, noel.

Noel, noel, noel
The truth we have to tell
He is born for to die
In a cold tomb to lie
No more on earth to sigh
Noel, noel, noel.

Noel, noel, noel
God has conquered hell
He has risen from the grave
Freely his own life he gave
Our eternal lives to save
Noel, noel, noel.

SONGS FROM A CHRISTMAS CAROL

F-O-G

The play, like the novel, starts in a penetrating, freezing cold fog. The cold permeates the streets and Scrooge's office

ALL: F-o-g f-o-g f-o-g f-o-g,
Seeping through the windows
Curling down the chimneys
Swirling round the lamps
Steaming from the ground
Muffling every sound
Blurring every lamp and post
Looming, looming like a ghost.
Cold bleak biting weather
Bites your toes, nips your nose
Makes you want to sleep for ever
Cold bleak biting weather
Can it really last for ever
Will the sun never come?
Cold bleak biting weather
Pouring in at ever crevice
Never been a greater menace.
Piercing searching biting cold
Gets through your vest
On to your chest

Makes you wheeze
And then you freeze
Can't see beyond your nose
And so you bang your toes
Already froze
And then you sneeze
And cough and wheeze
And stagger home
Through ice and snow
Cold bleak biting weather.

MERRY CHRISTMAS

Released from work, Bob Cratchit rushes home, going down a children's slide in the street 20 times in his relief to be going home for Christmas Day with his wife and children.

ALL: Merry Christmas, Merry Christmas, here we go,
       Merry Christmas, Merry Christmas, through the snow
       Though our feet are frozen and our hands are dropping off
       Still we feel like shouting till we lift the roof right off
       Merry Christmas, Merry Christmas, everyone.

ALL: Merry Christmas, Merry Christmas, sliding along
       Merry Christmas. Merry Christmas, first stop home
       Though we've got no money and our homes are very small
       Still we've got more warmth than the very biggest hall.
       Merry Christmas, Merry Christmas, everyone.

NEPHEW	Merry Christmas, Merry Christmas
SCROOGE	Humbug, humbug.
NEPHEW	Merry Christmas, Merry Christmas
SCROOGE	Humbug, bah!
NEPHEW	I'm sure that you don't mean it, for you can't have any reason To hate this marvellous, wonderful, this glorious season. Merry Christmas, Merry Christmas
SCROOGE	Humbug, bah!
NEPHEW	Merry Christmas, Merry Christmas
SCROOGE	Humbug, humbug! Humbug, bah! I've got no time for all these fools, I'm in a dreadful hurry It's time completely wasted, when I could be making money
NEPHEW	Merry Christmas, Merry Christmas
SCROOGE	Humbug, bah!

ALL   Merry Christmas, Merry Christmas,
presents for all
Merry Christmas, Merry Christmas, big
and small,
Though we can't buy caviar and bottles of
champagne
We'll have plum duff and lots of punch to
drink a toast again
To Merry Christmas, Merry Christmas
everyone.

THERE'S NOBODY HERE

Scrooge gets home from his office, makes his bowl of gruel, but is alarmed and thinks somebody may be in the house. He takes his candle and peers into several rooms – but 'there's nobody here' until suddenly there is.

SCROOGE: There's nobody here,
Nothing to fear,
Nobody under the table,
Nobody there at all,
Nobody under the sofa
However hard I call.

If I look so carefully
In every corner of every room
Though I walk so fearfully
Nothing can have any fear for me
– Oh!

There's nobody here
Nothing to fear
Nobody in the spare room
Nobody there at all
Nobody in the cupboard
However hard I call
If I double bolt every bolt
And double lock every lock
Then only a crazy dolt

Could ever think that he heard a
knock – What's that?

There's nobody here
Nothing to fear
Nobody underneath my bed
Nobody there at all
Nobody in my dressing gown
However hard I call
There's nobody in the basement
And nobody on the stairs
There's nobody in the building -
But what's happening to my hairs?

There's nobody here
Nothing to fear
No one behind the curtains
No one behind the chairs

Bells start ringing

Those house bells can't be ringing
Must be carollers singing

Chains clink and doors fly open

There can't be anything moving
If there is, it'd need much more proving

Marley's ghost enters and stands behind Scrooge

There's nobody here
Nothing to fear - - - ah!

Turns and see Marley's ghost, screams.

DREAMING

The Spirit of Christmas Past takes Scrooge into his own past life and he sees himself as a young boy and then a young man.
Scrooge as a boy is visited at his depressing boarding school by his little sister Fan, who comes to take him home for good.
They look forward to the future and sing of how it could be for them.

SCROOGE AS A BOY:
When I'm a man, I'd like to be a doctor
I'd like to cure and make sick children strong
For I can think of nothing finer
Than to right whatever has gone wrong

Chorus

SCROOGE AS A BOY AND FAN
Dreaming of a future
Dreaming of happiness
The world is our oyster
Let's go for the best.
Dreaming of a future
Of the pleasures on the way
The world is all before us
Let us start our lives today.

FAN

    Or p'raps you could become a famous writer
    And you could show grim scenes of modern life
    Go inside the prisons and the factories
    And try to end the sordid useless strife.

    Chorus

SCROOGE AS A BOY

    For men should live and work as brothers
    And try to help each other where they can,
    To make living a rich adventure
    That's what it means to be a man.

    Chorus

FAN   And when you find a girl who loves you.
    And who shares the ideals that you hold,
    You'll marry her and raise a family
    And find joy when you are old.

    Chorus

HAVING A BALL

The boss, where the young Scrooge is an apprentice,
throws a ball each Christmas for his employees.
Fezziwig, a happy, generous man, gives his workers a
night to remember.

We've got to put up up up the shutters
And sweep sweep sweep the floor,
Hang up the decorations
And the mistletoe over the door.
We've got to make the warehouse tidy
Make it warm from wall to wall,
Bring in the bowls of punch, boys,
We're going to have us a ball.

Bring in the boys from round the corner
And the girls from over the way
The ones who've never been here
And the ones who've been away
Bring in the young and the old together
Bring in the short ones and the tall,
Pick up your partners as they come, boys,
We're going to have us a ball.

Oh the ladies go into the centre
And then come out again
And the men go in and turn left
And take that girl in chain;
And you swing that girl around, boys
Then you let her go again,
And everybody promenades
Around that ring again.

FEZZIWIG

Although his workers all like and respect him, they sing a spoof song, claiming that he is a terrible, horrible employer.

CHORUS

>*Who do you think you'd like to go and work for?*
>*Fezziwig? He's one of the worst.*
>*Who do you think you'd like to dodge and shirk for?*
>*Fezziwig? You wouldn't durst.*

Oh, he don't mind if you're late each day,
If you sleep behind the shelves, or go out and play,
'Cos it only means he gives you no pay.
Fezziwig – that's him.

CHORUS

Oh, he doesn't make you stay to work late,
Miss your tea break, or break a date,
But if you don't – you're out of work, mate –
Fezziwig – that's him.

CHORUS

Oh, he's awfully kind to all of his staff,
And gives us music while we eat in his caf,
But ask for a rise – brother, that's a laugh.
Fezziwig – that's him.

CHORUS

Oh, he even runs a Christmas dance,
Where he brings his daughters to kick and
prance
But keep well away boys – no romance –
Fezziwig - that's him.

CHORUS

Oh, none of the things that we've sung about
Have really been true – he's not a lout –
To prove it boys let's give a shout
Fezziwig – that's not him.

FINAL CHORUS

Who do you really like to go and work for?
Fezziwig- he's one of the best
Who would you never ever dodge and shirk for?
Fezziwig – he's passed our test.
Oh, to show that we appreciate you
There's only one thing that we can do
Is to give you a present – from us to you –
Fezziwig for you.

Ending with presentation to Fezziwig of a special
gift

*The Spirit of Christmas Present shows Scrooge things
that are happening now around him*

<u>TEN SHOPPING HOURS TO CHRISTMAS</u>

*It is Christmas Eve, and the streets are crowded with last
minute shoppers, all looking for a bargain, all desperate
to finish their shopping and rush home to a roaring fire.
Shop-keepers are trying to tempt them with last-minute
bargains.*

CHORUS:

> *What a hurry, what a bustle
> We must rush and we must hustle
> Mind yourself and watch the bustle
> Buy quickly, buy.
> In and out this maddening throng
> Quicker now we can't stay long
> Spotting bargains for a song
> Buy quickly, buy.*
>
> *We must hurry, we must scurry
> What a state, we're much too late
> Rushing round we really hate
> Buy quickly, buy.
> Christmas wrapping, string and strapping
> In and out we're quickly popping.
> Finishing our Christmas shopping
> Buy quickly, buy.*

ALL: Ten shopping, nine shopping, eight shopping
        hours to Christmas

SHOP KEEPER:
        Buy a bird for twelve and three
        With each bird some stuffing free,
        Ten and nine, Nine and eight, eight and four,
        seven and three, three and five
        Half-a-crown
        Sold to the gentleman with the corporation
        – Who, me?

ALL: We must buy a new hat for Grandmama
        Not too audacious but curvaceous
        Warm and cosy with a posy
        In velour? How much more?
        Oh, I'm sure it's much nicer
        It will entice her
        Make her feel like a queen
        This hat we must buy for Grandmama.

CHORUS

ALL: Eight shopping, seven shopping, six shopping
        hours to Christmas

SHOP KEEPER:
>Tangerines at bargain price
>Sweet and juicy – very nice
>Ten and nine, Nine and eight, eight and
>four, seven and three, three and five
>Half-a-crown
>Sold to the lady with the scarlet petticoat
>- Who, me?

ALL: We must buy a new book for Auntie Maud
>Something haughty but not too naughty
>Not too sordid, for Aunt Maud'd
>Not approve. How about *Cranford*
>Something like *East Lynn* but not too thin.
>Nothing too shabby – try *Northanger Abbey*
>No – *A Christmas Carol* for dear Auntie Maud.

CHORUS

ALL: Six shopping, five shopping, four shopping hours
>to Christmas

SHOP KEEPER:
Get your bunch of mistletoe
Help to make your party go
Ten and nine, Nine and eight, eight and
four, seven and three,three and five
Half-a-crown
Sold to the gentleman attending to business –
- Who, me?

ALL: We must buy a long vest for Uncle Fred
Something to reach right down to his knees
Something to keep out the bitter freeze
Warm and woolly to cover his tummy
Manly, made in Hanley
Not Japanesey
But one joining comfort to ease
Is the vest we must buy for Uncle Fred.

CHORUS

ALL: Three shopping, two shopping, one shopping
hours to Christmas

SHOP KEEPER:

> Don't forget your rich port wine
> Brought from Venice, multo fine
> Ten and nine, Nine and eight, eight and
> four, seven and three, three and five
> Half-a-crown
> Sold to the lady adjusting her garter –
> -   Who, me?

ALL: I must buy some garters for Miss Betty Lee
> Do they come above or below the knee?
> Lacy and racy, flowered and frilly
> Not too slack and not too tight
> Keeping her stockings stretched just right
> Tested for stress and elasticity
> The garters we buy for Miss Betty Lee

CHORUS

ALL: No shopping, no shopping, no shopping hours to
Christmas.

MORE THAN ANY OTHER CHILD

Mrs Cratchit sings about her disabled child, Tiny Tim, and how she fears he will die.

He can't run about, like any other child
He can't jump and play, like any other child
He'll never kick a ball or skate or slide
Yet he seems to be so happy inside.

He's so delicate, unlike another child
But yet so good and kind, with such a thoughtful mind
He gets no better as the weeks and months go by
Please God – don't let him die.

He's so awfully small, unlike another child,
And hardly eats at all, unlike another child,
But yet I know as long as I shall live
That I love him, more than any other child.

ANIMAL QUIZ

Scrooge decides to visit his nephew and his wife on Christmas Day, much to the joy of Fred, and delightedly joins in a guessing game with all the young people at the party.

Is it a human being? No
Then it's a domestic pet? No
A wild beast from Africa, or something brought from Asia?
No, no, no.
It can't be stalking around? Yes
And really making a sound? Yes
Grunting and growling and yowling and howling?
Yes, yes, yes.

CHORUS:
You're making it all up
It just can't be true
There's no animal in the zoo
Could ever be like this.
Or seem like this
Oh, no, no, no, no, no, no, no.
I've never heard of anything
Quite like this ---

To audience ---have you?

Is it in a circus? No
Then in a market? No
It must be kept on a lead, or given a feed?
No, no, no.
It must be pulling a cart? No
Lining up at the start? No
Ranting and roaring and panting and pawing?
Yes. Yes, yes.

CHORUS:

It must be imaginary? No
It can't be real? Yes
A cow, a bull, a tiger, a dog, a pig, a cat?
No, no, no.
An ape, an ox, a marmoset, No
A stoat, a fox, a farmer's pet? No.
Strutting and prancing and kicking and dancing?
Yes, yes, yes.

CHORUS:

Has it got two eyes? Yes.
Has it got two ears? Yes
One nose, one mouth, two arms, two legs?
Yes, yes, yes.
Does it make a horrid sound? Yes
No heart ever been found? No
Fred – it is, it is, it is, it is –
Your Uncle Scrooge.
YES, YES, YES.

The Spirit of Christmas Future, a silent frightening figure, shows Scrooge scenes from the future.

MAKE A LITTLE MONEY

The Spirit of Christmas Future shows a bleak scene: a dingy pawnbroker's shop where three people bring the possessions of a dead Scrooge to try and make money by offering them for sale.

All: Money, money, get it where you can,
       Take it from a living or a dead, dead man
       If the man you rob is living,
       Then he's bound to say you're sinning
       But he's never quite as brave
       When he's lying in his grave –
       And the dead can't use it like the living
Chorus:
       Money, money, get it where you can,
       Take it from a living or a dead, dead man

Charwoman:
       Oh, it's hard cleaning steps for a ha'penny an hour

Launderess:
       Oh, it's hard washing clothes when we have to scrub and scour.

Undertaker:

>It's hard keeping my expression always grave and
>dour
>Knowing that the bloke who's gone had all the
>wealth and power

All: Now this man who's died got his money all
>through sinning
>But now he's dead and it's our turn to be
>winning

Chorus:

>*Make a little money where we can – Oh where
>we can.*
>*We've got to make a little money where we can.*

Undertaker:

>Here's his pencil case, 'cos he won't do no more
>writing
>Here's his buttons, 'cos his clothes won't need no
>tightening
>Here's a brooch wot his girlfriend give him long
> ago
>He's obeying her at last, when she told him
>where to go.
>And a seal or two that he used to press on letters
>He won't need 'em now, 'cos he's gone to join his
>betters

Chorus

Laundress:
> Here's his pure white towels, 'cos he won't do no
> more washing
> Here's his big black boots, 'cos he's finished his
> mud squashing
> Here's his sugar tongs, 'cos his tea won't need no
> sweetening
> And his silver spoons, 'cos he won't do no more
> stirring
> And his soft white sheets which I took without
> much weeping
> 'Cos wherever he is, I am sure he's through with
> sleeping.

Chorus

Charwoman:
> Here's his curtains took from the bed where he
> was lyin'
> And his blankets that can't warm him now he's
> fryin'
> His shirt of silk I took – when he wasn't listenin'
> 'Cos a shirt of calico is good enough to stiffen in
> In his lifetime he never gave away a thing
> Now he's dead, he gives his favours like a king

Chorus:
> *Make a little money where we can where we can*
> *We've got to make a little money where we can.*

48

MORE THAN ANY OTHER CHILD

(REPRISE - AMENDED)

We see the family mourning the death of Tiny Tim

He was so awfully small, unlike another child,
And hardly ate at all, unlike another child,
But yet I know as long as I shall live
That I love him, more than any other child.

He was so weak, my dears, unlike another child
But yet so patient and mild, unlike another child
And though his stay with us was very, very short
I still love him, more than any other child.

Back to the present time - no spirits now, only the overwhelming feeling of relief and joy.

MERRY CHRISTMAS

(REPRISE - AMENDED)

It is Christmas morning and Scrooge, overjoyed to find that it was all a dream but he is still here to do something about his way of life, celebrates.

ALL: Merry Christmas, Merry Christmas, here we go,
Merry Christmas, Merry Christmas, through the snow
Though our feet are frozen and our hands are dropping off
Still we feel like shouting till we lift the roof right off
Merry Christmas, Merry Christmas, everyone.

Merry Christmas, Merry Christmas, sliding along
Merry Christmas, Merry Christmas, first stop home
Though we've got no money and our homes are very small
Still we've got more warmth than the very biggest hall.
Merry Christmas, Merry Christmas, everyone

NEPHEW	Merry Christmas, Merry Christmas
SCROOGE	And to you, to you.
NEPHEW	Merry Christmas, Merry Christmas
SCROOGE	God bless you
	My boy, I really do mean it.
	I have every reason to love this
	marvellous, wonderful, glorious season.
NEPHEW	Merry Christmas, Merry Christmas
SCROOGE	Let's celebrate,
	Celebrate now.
	I've got time for all these people. I'm in
	no hurry
	It's time well spent, when I'm not making
	money.
ALL	Merry Christmas, Merry Christmas
	Merry Christmas, Merry Christmas,
	presents for all
	Merry Christmas, Merry Christmas, big
	and small,
	Though we can't buy caviar and bottles of
	champagne
	We'll have plum duff and lots of punch to
	drink a toast again.
	To Merry Christmas, Merry Christmas
	everyone.

DREAMING
(REPRISE)

The Cratchit family are welcomed by Scrooge to his office. Scrooge can see that Peter Cratchit will make a good partner in time.
The sign saying 'Scrooge and Marley' is removed and in its place is put 'Scrooge and Cratchit'.
Past, present and future all come together in a happy finale.

TINY TIM:

> When I'm a man, I'd like to be a doctor
> I'd like to cure and make sick children strong
> For I can think of nothing finer
> Than to right whatever has gone wrong

> *Chorus*

TINY TIM &SCROOGE

> *Dreaming of a future*
> *Dreaming of happiness*
> *The world is our oyster*
> *Let's go for the best.*
> *Dreaming of a future*
> *Of the pleasures on the way*
> *The world is all before us*
> *Let us start our lives today.*

SCROOGE

    Or p'raps you could become a famous writer
    And you could show grim scenes of modern life
    Go inside the prisons and the factories
    And try to end the sordid useless strife.

Chorus

TINY TIM

    For men should live and work as brothers
    And try to help each other where they can,
    To make living a rich adventure
    That's what it means to be a man.

Chorus

SCROOGE

    And when you find a girl who loves you.
    And who shares the ideals that you hold,
    You'll marry her and raise a family
    And find joy when you are old.

ALL: *Chorus*

BOOKS BY ERNIE RICHARDS

Celebrating Shakespeare

An anthology of some of the best of Shakespeare – speeches, scenes, sonnets and songs, together with an introduction, plus notes on every piece. The aim is to encourage everyone to speak these words aloud and share in the joy that Shakespeare's language brings us.

Shakespeare's Women in Love

A look at how Shakespeare presents the women in his plays. His position is not only that women are the equal of men, but he shows that they are superior to men in many aspects.

Blake's Jerusalem

The story of how *Jerusalem* came to be England's unofficial national anthem and the Women's Institute song: inspiring words by William Blake (1807) and thrilling music by Sir Hubert Parry (1915).

Makers of the Women's Institute

This book gives profiles of six fascinating pioneers in the WI movement: Adelaide Hoodless, Madge Watt, Lady Denman, Grace Hadow, Lady Brunner and Cecily McCall. All have a different but wonderful story to tell.

Resolution

This book lists people and events in WI history and in the social history of this country – books, speeches, resolutions and actions – that helped make life-changing improvements to the lives of women and their families.

I won't send roses

Poems trivial and serious, romantic and realistic, spanning a lifetime. The aim is to encourage everyone to write their own poems.

A Song for Christmas

Songs for and about Christmas, from a range of sources, mainly from a nativity play and a musical based on *A Christmas Carol* by Charles Dickens.

Straw in his hair

A nativity play based on 4 children's experiences at the time of Christ's birth. It involves them going to Bethlehem, greeting the new birth in the company of the shepherds and returning home transformed by the experience.

A Christmas Carol

Musical based on the novel by Dickens. All these songs arise naturally out of the marvellous language of the famous Dickens' story. They involve happiness, sadness, despair and transformation.

BOOKS BY JOHN HODGSON AND ERNIE RICHARDS

Improvisation (Methuen) 1966
A practical handbook on the uses of improvisation, both to create dramatic activities and its use to help bring alive existing texts.

Living Expression. Books 1 - 5 (Ginn) 1968 - 1971
A series of 5 books for secondary schools. The books contain a vast range of material, involving speech and movement work, acting, literature and current affairs. Each book includes an anthology of exciting literature and extracts from the press, radio and TV. A specially recorded LP accompanies each book, containing music, sounds and speeches to provide further stimuli.

Experience and expression (Ginn) 1968
A handbook for teachers exploring the range of activities in the 'Living Expression' books and ways of using the material.

BOOKS BY JOHN HODGSON

The Uses of Drama – Acting as a social and educational force (Methuen) 1977
An anthology, edited with extensive commentary by John Hodgson, of writings on drama and theatre.

Mastering movement: The Life and Work of Rudolf Laban (Methuen) 2001
His finest book.

John understood that movement was the heart of drama (as of life) and understanding this led him to research the life and work of Rudolf Laban, the great teacher and choreographer. Laban looked at movement in its infinite range, especially people in their normal lives and jobs, people in education and therapy, and people expressing themselves artistically, leading to an explosion of ideas in all forms of dance and drama, and in visual and sound designs.

Presenting Laban's often confusing ideas in an organised, comprehensive yet engrossing way is what John did superbly. What emerges is the enormous breadth of reference that Laban explored, encompassing movement study in every area of life and, through this, enhancing the potential of life for every individual.

ABOUT THE AUTHOR

Ernie Richards was born in Liverpool in 1927, and went to school at the Liverpool Institute (followed in the next decade by Paul McCartney)

He won a scholarship to Cambridge University, where he studied English, acted in various drama societies and ran the University Film Society.

During his National Service in the RAF he learned, and later, taught ballroom dancing at the Schofield School in Weston-Super-Mare.

For the Liverpool Theatre Guild, he wrote, with Esther Graham, and directed a revue called *To crown it all* to celebrate the Coronation of Queen Elizabeth II.

He met John Hodgson and for 10 years, in the sixties, they worked on occasional drama courses and wrote 7 books together. They then pursued their separate careers, but the influence of John on Ernie was deep and lasting.

For many years, he taught English and drama at the I M Marsh College of Physical Education in Liverpool.

He directed a wide range of plays there, including: *The Rape of the Locks,* (by Menander) *Antigone* (Sophocles and Anouilh) *The Trojan Women, Faustus, A Midsummer*

Night's Dream, a reconstructed first night of *Twelfth Night,* collage versions of *Hamlet* and *King Lear; Peer Gynt* and *Brand, An Italian Straw Hat, The Threepenny Opera* and *The Marat/Sade.*

He founded and ran Group Theatre Liverpool, with Ken Jones and Sheila Fay. They did a range of plays, all in the round – Stephen Joseph was a very powerful advocate - including the first production on Merseyside of a Brecht play, *The Caucasian Chalk Circle* at the Neptune Theatre.

He also founded the Liverpool Youth Theatre. First members included Alison Steadman, Bill Stewart and Tony Haygarth. First productions were *Listen to the Wind, Dark of the Moon,* and *The Doctor and the Devils.*

He took his production of *Faustus* to the Liverpool Playhouse and he directed *Turandot* at the Royal Court Liverpool and *Noye's Fludde* at Liverpool Cathedral.

He directed a new play at the Playhouse Upstairs and a summer season of plays at Aberystwyth, including Chekhov and Michael Frayn.

He later became Principal of Urchfont Manor Adult Residential College in Wiltshire.

He initiated many new courses including certificate and diploma courses, including in drama. He helped Brian Cory to create Job Force Theatre in the stable yard of the College, for unemployed young people. Another group from Job Force built extra rooms out of the run-down stable yard buildings. This acting group made a deep impression on the youngsters involved and everybody who saw them, as they toured local schools. The group had talented leaders, led by Brian and including Peter Safka (music) and Kim (movement and dance).

He directed *Comedy of Errors* and *Lock up your daughters* for the Wharf Theatre, Devizes.

Now retired, he lives in Norfolk.

Published by Ernie Richards, Springwood, Church Lane, Sparham, Norwich NR9 5PP 01362 688543

ernierich@hotmail.com

Cover:
The painting: Bruegel the Elder: Winter scene with skaters and bird trap.
The design: Martin Richards

Printed in Great Britain
by Amazon

40337768R00036